ROCK-A-BYE BABY QUILTS

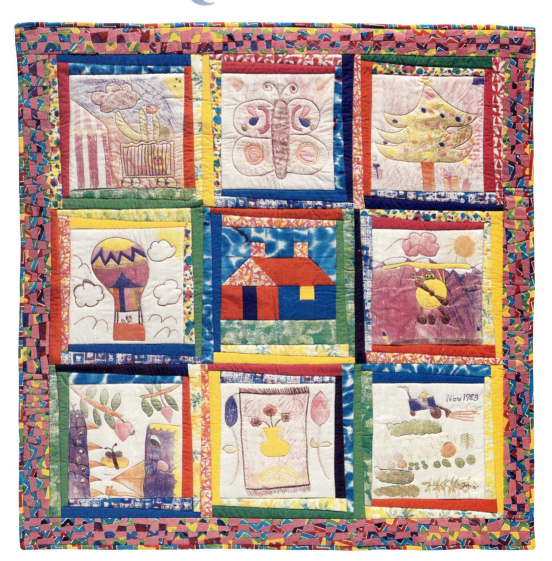

Oxmoor House ®

ROCK-A-BYE BABY QUILTS

©1996 by Oxmoor House, Inc.

Book Division of Southern Progress Corporation
P.O. Box 2463, Birmingham, AL 35201

Published by Oxmoor House, Inc., and
Leisure Arts, Inc.

Library of Congress Catalog Number: 96-067097
ISBN: 0-8487-1282-X

Manufactured in the United States of America
First Printing 1996

Editor-in-Chief: Nancy Fitzpatrick Wyatt
Editorial Director, Special Interest Publications:
  Ann H. Harvey
Senior Crafts Editor: Susan Ramey Cleveland
Senior Editor, Editorial Services: Olivia Kindig Wells
Art Director: James Boone

ROCK-A-BYE BABY QUILTS

Editor: Catherine Corbett Fowler
Editorial Assistant: Barzella Estle
Copy Editor: Karla Price Higgs
Senior Designer: Larry Hunter
Designer: Carol Loria
Illustrator: Kelly Davis
Publishing Systems Administrator: Rick Tucker
Senior Photographer: John O'Hagan
Photo Stylist: Katie Stoddard
Production and Distribution Director: Phillip Lee
Associate Production Managers: Theresa L. Beste,
  Vanessa D. Cobbs
Production Coordinator: Marianne Jordan Wilson
Production Assistant: Valerie L. Heard

Contents

Dear Quilting Friends,

Perhaps the most cherished quilts of all are those made for little ones. Here are 10 small wonders you can make for an upcoming blessed event or for any special child in your life. Just as babies and children are fun, the quilts in this book are fun to make, containing special techniques and heartwarming surprises.

Turn to page 12 to learn the secret hidden in Georgia Bonesteel's *Peekaboo* quilt. Embroider Carol Tipton's endearing characters to embellish the *Noah's Star* quilt on page 39. Use the old-fashioned technique of string piecing to make Dorothy Winkeljohn's *Calico Strings* on page 26. Let your child create her own original art to showcase in your version of Katy Widger's *Child's Play* on page 20.

These quilts were designed to be used and loved by the children who receive them. They're also special enough to become family heirlooms long after the children have grown to be adults.

Happy stitching,

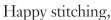

Page 12

WORKSHOP

Selecting Fabrics

The best fabric for quilts is 100% cotton. Yardage requirements are based on 44"-wide fabric and allow for shrinkage. All fabrics, including backing, should be machine-washed, dried, and pressed before cutting. Use warm water and detergent but not fabric softener.

Necessary Notions

- Scissors
- Rotary cutter and mat
- Acrylic rulers
- Template plastic
- Pencils for marking cutting lines
- Sewing needles
- Sewing thread
- Sewing machine
- Seam ripper
- Pins
- Iron and ironing board
- Quilting needles
- Thimble
- Hand quilting thread
- Machine quilting thread

Making Templates

A template is a duplication of a printed pattern, made from a sturdy material, which is traced onto fabric. Many regular shapes such as squares and triangles can be marked directly on the fabric with a ruler, but you need templates for other shapes. Some quiltmakers use templates for all shapes.

You can trace patterns directly onto template plastic. Or make a template by tracing a pattern onto graph paper and gluing the paper to posterboard or sandpaper. (Sandpaper will not slip on fabric.)

When a large pattern is given in two pieces, make one template for the complete piece.

Cut out the template on the marked line. It is important that a template be traced, marked, and cut accurately. If desired, punch out corner dots with a 1/8"-diameter hole punch (Diagram 1).

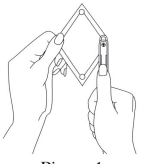

Diagram 1

Mark each template with its letter and grain line. Verify the template's accuracy, placing it over the printed pattern. Any discrepancy, however small, is multiplied many times as the quilt is assembled. Another way to check templates' accuracy is to make a test block before cutting more pieces.

Tracing Templates on Fabric

For hand piecing, templates should be cut to the finished size of the piece so seam lines can be marked on the fabric. Avoiding the selvage, place the template *facedown* on the *wrong* side of the fabric, aligning the template grain line with the straight grain. Hold the template firmly and trace around it. Repeat as needed, leaving 1/2" between tracings (**Diagram 2**).

Diagram 2

For machine piecing, templates should include seam allowances. These templates are used in the same manner as for hand piecing, but you can mark the fabric using common lines for efficient cutting (**Diagram 3**). Mark corners on fabric through holes in the template.

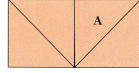

Diagram 3

For hand or machine piecing, use window templates to enhance accuracy by drawing and cutting out both cutting and sewing lines. The guidance of a drawn seam line is very useful for sewing set-in seams, when pivoting at a precise point is critical. Used on the right side of the fabric, window templates help you cut specific motifs with accuracy (**Diagram 4**).

Diagram 4

For hand appliqué, templates should be made the finished size. Place templates *faceup* on the *right* side of the fabric. Position tracings at least 1/2" apart (**Diagram 5**). Add a 1/4" seam allowance around pieces when cutting.

Diagram 5

Cutting

Grain Lines

Woven threads form the fabric's grain. Lengthwise grain, parallel to the selvages, has the least stretch; crosswise grain has a little more give.

Long strips such as borders should be cut lengthwise whenever possible and cut first to ensure that you have the necessary length. Usually, other pieces can be cut aligned with either grain.

Bias is the 45° diagonal line between the two grain directions. Bias has the most stretch and is used for curving strips such as flower stems. Bias is often preferred for binding.

Never use the selvage (finished edge). Selvage does not react to washing, drying, and pressing like the rest of the fabric and may pucker when the finished quilt is laundered.

Rotary Cutting

A rotary cutter, used with a protective mat and a ruler, takes getting used to but is very efficient for cutting strips, squares, and triangles. A rotary cutter is fast because you can measure and cut multiple layers with a single stroke, without templates or marking. It is also more accurate than cutting with scissors because fabrics remain flat and do not move during cutting.

Because the blade is very sharp, be sure to get a rotary cutter with a safety guard. Keep the guard in the safe position at all times, except when making a cut. *Always keep the cutter out of the reach of children.*

Use the cutter with a self-healing mat. A good mat for cutting strips is at least 23" wide.

1. Squaring the fabric is the first step in accurate cutting. Fold the fabric with selvages aligned. With the yardage to your right, align a small square ruler with the fold near the cut edge. Place a long ruler against the left side of the square (**Diagram 6**). Keeping the long ruler in place, remove the square. Hold the ruler in place with your left hand as you cut, rolling the cutter *away from you* along the ruler's edge with a steady motion. You can move your left hand along the ruler as you cut, but do not change the position of the ruler. *Keep your fingers away from the ruler's edge when cutting.*

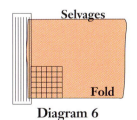

Selvages

Fold

Diagram 6

2. Open the fabric. If the cut was not accurately perpendicular to the fold, the edge will be V-shaped instead of straight (**Diagram 7**). Correct the cut if necessary.

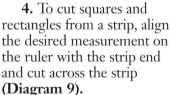

Correct cut

Not cut at 90° angle

Fold

Diagram 7

3. With a transparent ruler, you can measure and cut at the same time. Fold the fabric in half again, aligning the selvages with the fold, making four layers that line up perfectly along the cut edge. Project instructions designate the strip width needed. Position the ruler to measure the correct distance from the edge (**Diagram 8**) and cut. The blade will easily cut through all four layers. Check the strip to be sure the cut is straight. The strip length is the width of the fabric, approximately 43" to 44". Using the ruler again, trim selvages, cutting about ⅜" from each end.

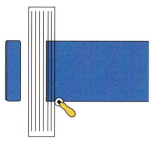

Diagram 8

4. To cut squares and rectangles from a strip, align the desired measurement on the ruler with the strip end and cut across the strip (**Diagram 9**).

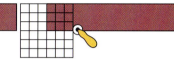

Diagram 9

5. Cut triangles from squares or rectangles. Cutting instructions often direct you to cut a square in half or in quarters diagonally to make right triangles, and this technique can apply to rectangles, too (**Diagram 10**). The outside edges of the square or rectangle are on the straight of the grain, so triangle sides cut on the diagonal are bias.

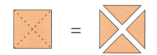

Diagram 10

6. Some projects in this book use a time-saving technique called strip piecing. With this method, strips are joined to make a pieced band. Cut across the seams of this band to cut preassembled units (**Diagram 11**).

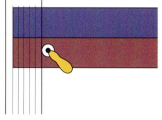

Diagram 11

Machine Piecing

Your sewing machine does not have to be a new, computerized model. A good straight stitch is all that's necessary, but it may be helpful to have a nice satin stitch for appliqué. Clean and oil your machine regularly, use good-quality thread, and replace needles frequently.

1. Patches for machine piecing are cut with the seam allowance included, but the sewing line is not usually marked. Therefore, a way to make a consistent ¼" seam is essential. Some presser feet have a right toe that is ¼" from the needle. Other machines have an adjustable needle that can be set for a ¼" seam. If your machine has neither feature, experiment to find how the fabric must be placed to make a ¼" seam. Mark this position on the presser foot or throat plate.

2. Use a stitch length that makes a strong seam but is not too difficult to remove with a seam ripper. The best setting is usually 10 to 12 stitches per inch.

3. Pin only when really necessary. If a straight seam is less than 4" and does not have to match an adjoining seam, pinning is not necessary.

4. When intersecting seams must align **(Diagram 12),** match the units with right sides facing and push a pin through both seams at the seam line. Turn the pinned unit to the right side to check the alignment; then pin securely. As you sew, remove each pin just before the needle reaches it.

Figure 1   Figure 2

Intersecting seams aligned   Intersecting seams not aligned

Diagram 12

5. Block assembly diagrams are used throughout this book to show how pieces should be joined. Make small units first; then join them in rows and continue joining rows to finish the block **(Diagram 13).** Blocks are joined in the same manner to complete the quilt top.

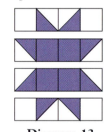

Diagram 13

6. Chain piecing saves time. Stack pieces to be sewn in pairs, with right sides facing. Join the first pair as usual. At the end of the seam, do not backstitch, cut the thread, or lift the presser foot. Just feed in the next pair of pieces—the machine will make a few stitches between pieces before the needle strikes the second piece of fabric. Continue sewing in this way until all pairs are joined. Stack the chain of pieces until you are ready to clip them apart **(Diagram 14).**

Diagram 14

7. Most seams are sewn straight across, from raw edge to raw edge. Since they will be crossed by other seams, they do not require backstitching to secure them.

8. When piecing diamonds or other angled seams, you may need to make set-in seams. For these, always mark the corner dots (shown on the patterns) on the fabric pieces. Stitch one side, starting at the outside edge and being careful not to sew beyond the dot into the seam allowance **(Diagram 15, Figure A).** Backstitch. Align the other side of the piece as needed, with right sides facing. Sew from the dot to the outside edge **(Figure B).**

9. Sewing curved seams requires extra care. First, mark the centers of both the convex (outward) and concave (inward) curves **(Diagram 16).** Staystitch just inside the seam allowance of both pieces. Clip the concave piece to the stitching **(Figure A).** With right sides facing and raw edges aligned, pin the two patches together at the center **(Figure B)** and at the left edge **(Figure C).** Sew from edge to center, stopping frequently to check that the raw edges are aligned. Stop at the center with the needle down. Raise the presser foot and pin the pieces together from the center to the right edge. Lower the foot and continue to sew. Press seam allowances toward the concave curve **(Figure D).**

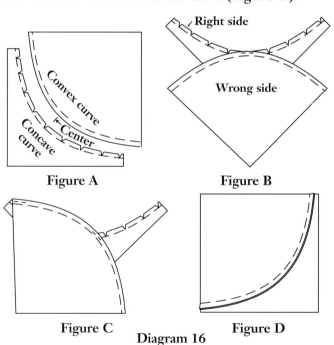

Figure A   Figure B

Figure C   Figure D

Diagram 16

Hand Piecing

Make a running stitch of 8 to 10 stitches per inch along the marked seam line on the wrong side of the fabric. Don't pull the fabric as you sew; let the pieces lie relaxed in your hand. Sew from seam line to seam line, not from edge to edge as in machine piecing.

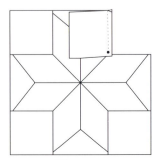 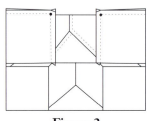

Figure 1   Figure 2

Diagram 15

When ending a line of stitching, backstitch over the last stitch and make a loop knot **(Diagram 17)**.

Diagram 17

Match seams and points accurately, pinning patches together before piecing. Align match points as described in Step 4 under Machine Piecing.

When joining units where several seams meet, do not sew over seam allowances; sew *through* them at the match point **(Diagram 18)**. When four or more seams meet, press the seam allowances in the same direction to reduce bulk **(Diagram 19)**.

Diagram 18

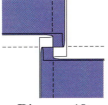

Diagram 19

Pressing

Careful pressing is necessary for precise piecing. Press each seam as you go. Sliding the iron back and forth may push the seam out of shape. Use an up-and-down motion, lifting the iron from spot to spot. Press the seam flat on the wrong side. Open the piece and, on the right side, press both seam allowances to one side (usually toward the darker fabric). Pressing the seam open leaves tiny gaps through which batting may beard.

Appliqué

Traditional Hand Appliqué

Hand appliqué requires that you turn under a seam allowance around the shape to prevent frayed edges.

1. Trace around the template on the right side of the fabric. This line indicates where to turn the seam allowance. Cut each piece approximately ¼" outside the line.

2. For simple shapes, turn the edges by pressing the seam allowance to the back; complex shapes may require basting the seam allowance. Sharp points and strong curves are best appliquéd with freezer paper. Clip curves to make a smooth edge. With practice, you can work without pressing seam allowances, turning edges under with the needle as you sew.

3. Do not turn under any seam allowance that will be covered by another appliqué piece.

4. To stitch, use one strand of cotton-wrapped polyester sewing thread in a color that matches the appliqué. Use a slipstitch, but keep the stitch very small on the surface. Working from right to left (or left to right if you're left-handed), pull the needle through the

base fabric and catch only a few threads on the folded edge of the appliqué. Reinsert the needle into the base fabric, under the top thread on the appliqué edge to keep the thread from tangling **(Diagram 20)**.

5. An alternative to slipstitching is to work a decorative buttonhole stitch around each figure **(Diagram 21)**.

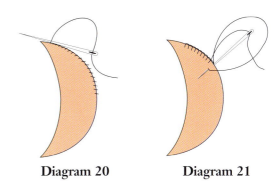

Diagram 20   **Diagram 21**

Freezer Paper Hand Appliqué

Supermarket freezer paper saves time because it eliminates the need for basting seam allowances.

1. Trace the template onto the *dull* side of the freezer paper and cut the paper on the marked line. *Note:* If a design is not symmetrical, turn the template over and trace a mirror image so the fabric piece won't be reversed when you cut it out.

2. Pin the freezer-paper shape, with its *shiny side* up, to the *wrong side* of the fabric. Following the paper shape and adding a scant ¼" seam allowance, cut out the fabric piece. Do not remove pins.

3. Using just the tip of a dry iron, press the seam allowance to the shiny side of the paper. Be careful not to touch the freezer paper with the iron.

4. Appliqué the piece to the background as in traditional appliqué. Trim the fabric from behind the shape, leaving ¼" seam allowances. Separate the freezer paper from the fabric with your fingernail and pull gently to remove it. If you prefer not to trim the background fabric, pull out the freezer paper before you complete stitching.

5. Sharp points require special attention. Turn the point down and press it **(Diagram 22, Figure A)**. Fold the seam allowance on one side over the point and press **(Figure B)**; then fold the other seam allowance over the point and press **(Figure C)**.

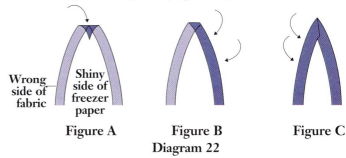

Wrong side of fabric   Shiny side of freezer paper

Figure A   **Figure B**   **Figure C**

Diagram 22

6. When pressing curved edges, clip sharp inward curves **(Diagram 23)**. If the shape doesn't curve smoothly, separate the paper from the fabric with your fingernail and try again.

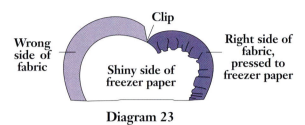

Diagram 23

7. Remove the pins when all seam allowances have been pressed to the freezer paper. Position the prepared appliqué right side up on the background fabric. Press to adhere it to the background fabric.

Machine Appliqué

A machine-sewn satin stitch makes a neat edging. For machine appliqué, cut appliqué pieces without adding seam allowances.

Using fusible web to adhere pieces to the background adds a stiff extra layer to the appliqué and is not appropriate for some quilts. It is best used on small pieces, difficult fabrics, or for wall hangings and accessories in which added stiffness is acceptable. The web prevents fraying and shifting during appliqué.

Place tear-away stabilizer under the background fabric behind the appliqué. Machine-stitch the appliqué edges with a satin stitch or close-spaced zigzag **(Diagram 24)**. Test the stitch length and width on a sample first. Use an open-toed presser foot. Remove the stabilizer when appliqué is complete.

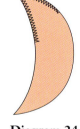

Diagram 24

Measuring Borders

Because seams may vary and fabrics may stretch a bit, opposite sides of your assembled quilt top may not be the same measurement. You can (and should) correct this when you add borders.

Measure the length of each side of the quilt. Trim the side border strips to match the *shorter* of the two sides. Join borders to the quilt as described below, easing the longer side of the quilt to fit the border. Join borders to the top and bottom edges in the same manner.

Straight Borders

Side borders are usually added first **(Diagram 25)**. With right sides facing and raw edges aligned, pin the center of one border strip to the center of one side of

Diagram 25

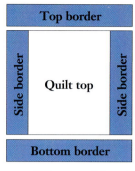

Diagram 26

the quilt top. Pin the border to the quilt at each end and then pin along the side as desired. Machine-stitch with the border strip on top. Press the seam allowance toward the border. Trim excess border fabric at each end. In the same manner, add the border to the opposite side and then the top and bottom borders **(Diagram 26)**.

Mitered Borders

1. Measure your quilt sides. Trim the side border strips to fit the shorter side *plus* the width of the border *plus* 2".

2. Center the measurement of the shorter side on one border strip, placing a pin at each end and at the center of the measurement.

3. With right sides facing and raw edges aligned, match the pins on the border strip to the center and corners of the longer side of the quilt. (Border fabric will extend beyond the corners.)

4. Start machine-stitching at the top pin, backstitching to lock the stitches. Continue to sew, easing the quilt between pins. Stop at the last pin and backstitch. Join remaining borders in the same manner. Press seam allowances toward borders.

5. With right sides facing, fold the quilt diagonally, aligning the raw edges of adjacent borders. Pin securely **(Diagram 27)**.

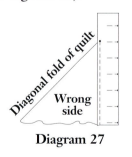

Diagram 27

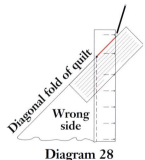

Diagram 28

6. Align a yardstick or quilter's ruler along the diagonal fold **(Diagram 28)**. Holding the ruler firmly, mark a line from the end of the border seam to the raw edge.

7. Start machine-stitching at the beginning of the marked line, backstitch, and then stitch on the line out to the raw edge.

8. Unfold the quilt to be sure that the corner lies flat. Correct the stitching if necessary. Trim the seam allowance to ¼".

9. Miter the remaining corners in the same manner. Press the corner seams open.

Quilting Without Marking

Some quilts can be quilted in-the-ditch (right along the seam line), outline-quilted (¼" from the seam line), or echo-quilted (lines of quilting rippling outward from the design like waves on a pond). These methods can be used without any marking at all. If you are machine quilting, simply use the edge of your presser foot and the seam line as a guide. If you are hand quilting, by the time you have pieced a quilt top, your eye will be practiced enough for you to produce straight, even quilting without the guidance of marked lines.

Marking Quilting Designs

Many quilters like to mark the entire top at one time, a practice that requires long-lasting markings. The most common tool for this purpose is a sharp **pencil.** However, most pencils are made with an oil-based graphite lead, which often will not wash out completely. Look for a high-quality artist's pencil marked "2H" or higher (the higher the number, the harder the lead, and the lighter the line it will make). Sharpen the pencil frequently to keep the line on the fabric thin and light. Or try a mechanical pencil with a 0.5-mm lead. It will maintain a fine line without sharpening.

While you are in the art supply store, get a **white plastic eraser** (brand name Magic Rub). This eraser, used by professional drafters and artists, will cleanly remove the carbon smudges left by pencil lead without fraying the fabric or leaving eraser crumbs.

Water- and **air-soluble marking pens** are convenient, but controversial, marking tools. Some quilters have found that the marks reappear, often up to several years later, while others have no problems with them.

Be sure to test these pens on each fabric you plan to mark and *follow package directions exactly.* Because the inks can be permanently set by heat, be very careful with a marked quilt. Do not leave it in your car on a hot day and never touch it with an iron until the marks have been removed. Plan to complete the quilting within a year after marking it with a water-soluble pen.

Air-soluble pens are best for marking small sections at a time. The marks disappear within 24 to 48 hours, but the ink remains in the fabric until it is washed. After the quilt is completed and before it is used, rinse it twice in clear, cool water, using no soap, detergent, or bleach. Let the quilt air-dry.

For dark fabrics, the cleanest marker you can use is a thin sliver of pure, white **soap.** Choose a soap that contains no creams, deodorants, dyes, or perfumes; these added ingredients may leave a residue on the fabric.

Other marking tools include **colored pencils** made specifically for marking fabric and **tailor's chalk** (available in powdered, stick, and traditional cake form). When using chalk, mark small sections of the quilt at a time because the chalk rubs off easily.

Quilting Stencils

Quilting patterns can be purchased as precut stencils. Simply lay these on your quilt top and mark the design through the cutout areas.

To make your own stencil of a printed quilting pattern, such as the one below, use a permanent marker to trace the design onto a blank sheet of template plastic. Then use a craft knife to cut out the design.

Quilting Stencil Pattern

Making a Quilt Backing

Some fabric and quilt shops sell 90" and 108" widths of 100% cotton fabric that are very practical for quilt backing. However, the instructions in this book always give backing yardage based on 44"-wide fabric.

When using 44"-wide fabric, all quilts wider than 41" will require a pieced backing. For quilts 41" to 80" wide, you will need an amount of fabric equal to two times the desired *length* of the unfinished backing. (The unfinished backing should be at least 3" larger on all sides than the quilt top.)

The simplest method of making a backing is to cut the fabric in half widthwise **(Diagram 29),** and then sew the two panels together lengthwise. This results in a backing with a vertical center seam. Press the seam allowances to one side.

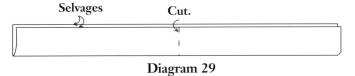

Diagram 29

Another method of seaming the backing results in two vertical seams and a center panel of fabric. This method is often preferred by quilt show judges. Begin by cutting the fabric in half widthwise. Open the two lengths and stack them, with right sides facing and selvages aligned. Stitch along *both* selvage edges to create a tube of fabric **(Diagram 30).** Cut down the center of the top layer of fabric only and open the fabric flat **(Diagram 31).** Press seam allowances to one side.

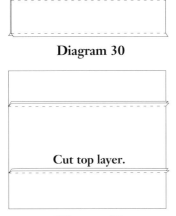

Diagram 30

Cut top layer.

Diagram 31

If the quilt is wider than 80", it is more economical to cut the fabric into three lengths that are the desired width of the backing. Join the three lengths so that the seams are horizontal to the quilt, rather than vertical. For this method, you'll need an amount of fabric equal to three times the *width* of the unfinished backing.

Fabric requirements in this book reflect the most economical method of seaming the backing fabric.

Layering and Basting

After the quilt top and backing are made, the next steps are layering and basting in preparation for quilting.

Prepare a large working surface to spread out the quilt—a large table, two tables pushed together, or the floor. Place the backing on the working surface wrong side up. Unfold the batting and place it on top of the backing, smoothing away any wrinkles or lumps.

Lay the quilt top wrong side down on top of the batting and backing. Make sure the edges of the backing and quilt top are parallel.

Knot a long strand of sewing thread and use a long (darning) needle for basting. Begin basting in the center of the quilt and baste out toward the edges. The basting stitches should cover an ample amount of the quilt so that the layers do not shift during quilting.

Machine quilters use nickel-plated safety pins for basting so there will be no basting threads to get caught on the presser foot. Safety pins, spaced approximately 4" apart, can be used by hand quilters, too.

Hand Quilting

Hand-quilted stitches should be evenly spaced, with the spaces between stitches about the same length as the stitches themselves. The *number* of stitches per inch is less important than the *uniformity* of the stitching. Don't worry if you take only five or six stitches per inch; just be consistent throughout the project.

Machine Quilting

For machine quilting, the backing and batting should be 3" larger all around than the quilt top, because the quilting process pushes the quilt top fabric outward. After quilting, trim the backing and batting to the same size as the quilt top.

Thread your bobbin with good-quality sewing thread (not quilting thread) in a color to match the backing. Use a top thread color to match the quilt top or use invisible nylon thread.

An even-feed or walking foot will feed all the quilt's layers through the machine at the same speed. It is possible to machine-quilt without this foot (by experimenting with tension and presser foot pressure), but it will be much easier *with* it. If you do not have this foot, get one from your sewing machine dealer.

Straight-Grain Binding

1. Mark the fabric in horizontal lines the width of the binding (**Diagram 32**).

A	↕ width of binding	
B		A
C		B
D		C
E		D
F		E
		F

Diagram 32

2. With right sides facing, fold the fabric in half, offsetting drawn lines by matching letters and raw edges (**Diagram 33**). Stitch a ¼" seam.

3. Cut the binding in a continuous strip, starting with one end and following the marked lines around the tube. Press the strip in half lengthwise.

Diagram 33

Continuous Bias Binding

This technique can be used to make continuous bias for appliqué as well as for binding.

1. Cut a square of fabric in half diagonally to form two triangles. With right sides facing, join the triangles (**Diagram 34**). Press the seam allowance open.

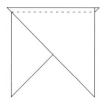

Diagram 34

2. Mark parallel lines the desired width of the binding (**Diagram 35**), taking care not to stretch the bias. With right sides facing, align the raw edges (indicated as Seam 2). As you align the edges, offset one Seam 2 point past its natural matching point by one line. Stitch the seam; then press the seam allowance open.

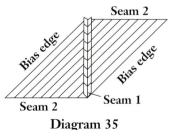

Diagram 35

3. Cut the binding in a continuous strip, starting with the protruding point and following the marked lines around the tube (**Diagram 36**). Press the strip in half lengthwise.

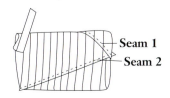

Diagram 36

Applying Binding

Binding is applied to the front of the quilt first. You may begin anywhere on the edge of the quilt except at the corner.

1. Matching raw edges, lay the binding on the quilt. Fold down the top corner of the binding at a 45° angle, align the raw edges, and pin (**Diagram 37**).

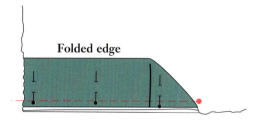

Folded edge

Diagram 37

2. Beginning at the folded end, machine-stitch the binding to the quilt. Stop stitching ¼" from the corner and backstitch. Fold the binding strip diagonally away from the quilt, making a 45° angle (**Diagram 38**).

3. Fold the binding strip straight down along the next side to be stitched, creating a pleat in the corner. Position the needle at the ¼" seam line of the new side (**Diagram 39**). Make a few stitches, backstitch, and then stitch the seam. Continue until all corners and sides are done. Overlap the end of the binding strip over the beginning fold and stitch about 2" beyond it. Trim any excess binding.

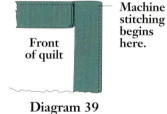

Front of quilt

Machine stitching begins here.

Diagram 38

Diagram 39

4. Turn the binding over the raw edge of the quilt. Slipstitch it in place on the back, using thread that matches the binding. The fold at the beginning of the binding strip will create a neat, angled edge when it is folded to the back.

5. At each corner, fold the binding to form a miter (**Diagram 40**). Hand-stitch the miters closed if desired.

Back of quilt

Diagram 40

Quilt by Georgia Bonesteel
Hendersonville, North Carolina

Peekaboo

Use motifs cut from novelty prints for several of the center squares to create this playful *Peekaboo* quilt. Solid fabric flaps sewn right into the patchwork seam will keep your secret hidden. Hidden, that is, until an inquisitive child pulls the flap back to reveal a pink pig or a buzzing bee or perhaps even a cow on roller skates!

Finished Quilt Size

52" square

Number of Blocks and Finished Size

8 blocks   12" square

Fabric Requirements

Green solid	¾ yard
Yellow solid	¾ yard
Coordinating stripe	⅞ yard
Coordinating print	⅞ yard
Whimsical prints*	scraps
Backing	3 yards

*Novelty prints are for hidden squares.

Other Materials

Baby or sport weight yarn
Yarn needle

Number to Cut

Template A	12 green solid	
	12 yellow solid	
Template B	48 green solid	
	48 yellow solid	
Template C	24 coordinating stripe	
	24 coordinating print	

Quilt Top Assembly

1. Referring to **Block Assembly Diagram,** join 1 green A to 4 yellow Bs. Repeat. Join 1 yellow A to 4 green Bs. Arrange 3 A/B squares, 3 striped Cs and 3 print Cs in 3 vertical rows, as shown. Stitch together vertical rows. Join rows. Repeat process to make a total of 8 blocks, referring to

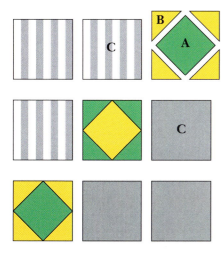

Block Assembly Diagram

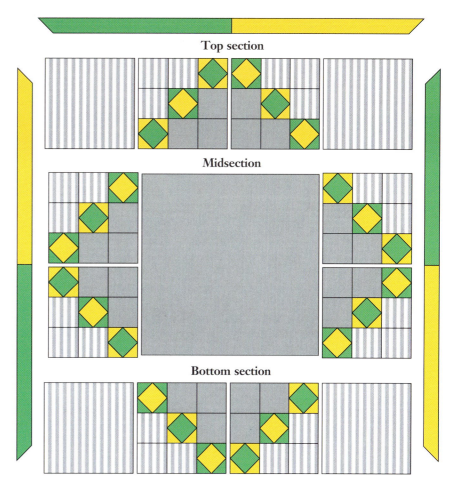

Setting Diagram

Setting Diagram for color placement of A and B Templates. *Note:* Before completing all 8 blocks, see Step 2 for incorporating hidden squares.

2. To make hidden square, replace green or yellow As, as desired, with whimsical print As. Make a covering flap for each whimsical print A by stitching 2 green (or yellow) As, right sides facing, along 3 edges. Turn. Insert raw edge of flap into seam between whimsical print A and a neighboring B. (*Tip:* Set needle at half-right position or shift piecing slightly to make the seam allowance a bit smaller, allowing the flap to set in nicely.)

3. For top section of quilt, join 1 (12½") stripe square to each side of 2 pieced blocks. (See **Setting Diagram.**) Repeat for bottom section of quilt. For midsection of quilt, join 2 pieced blocks to each

side of 1 (24½") coordinating print square. Join top section, midsection, and bottom section of quilt.

4. Cut 4 (2½" x 26½") strips each from green and yellow solids. Referring to **Setting Diagram,** join 1 green and 1 yellow strip along 1 short end. Repeat to make a total of 4 border strips. Join border strips to quilt, mitering corners.

5. Layer batting; top, right side up; and backing, right side down. With batting against feed dogs, join layers along sides and bottom, leaving an opening for turning. Turn, with batting on inside. Slipstitch opening closed. Edgestitch ¼" from edges.

Quilting

Cut yarn into 12" lengths. Thread yarn needle with 1 length of yarn. Sew yarn through all thicknesses and tie on top. Continue tying quilt as desired.

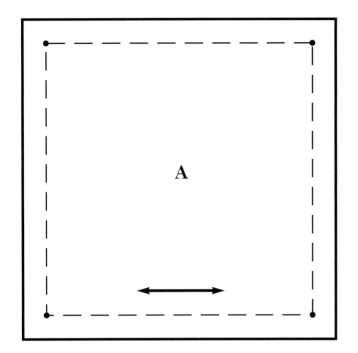

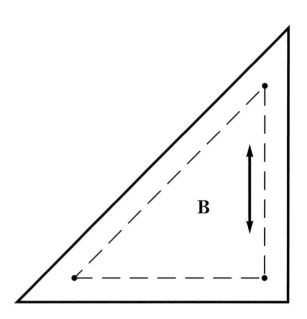

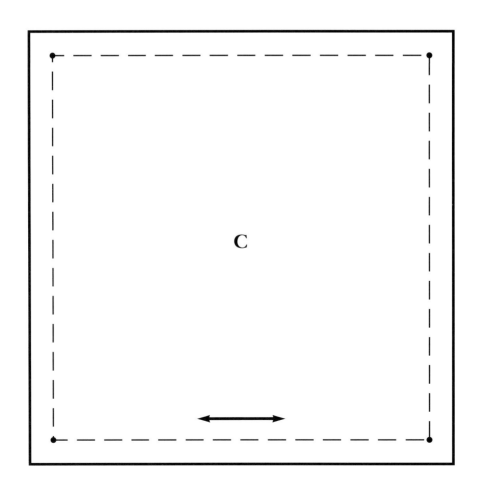

Quilt by Joyce a'Lora Neal
Chehalis, Washington

Shadow of Her Smile

"If I could accomplish anything with quiltmaking," says Joyce a'Lora Neal, "it would be to lift baby quilts to their rightful place as priceless treasures and heirlooms." Having made several shadow-appliquéd quilts, Joyce has found that "quilting-as-you-appliqué" works best for her, even on one-piece quilts. She recommends this method because of the unstable nature of voile.

Finished Quilt Size
38" x 53"

Fabric Requirements
White   1¾ yards
White voile   1¾ yards
Light blue   ⅛ yard
White for
  backing   1¾ yards

Other Materials
Braid, white with flower design
  for oval   1⅝ yards
Braid, white for
  first frame   3¼ yards
Braid, white for
  second frame 4⅝ yards

Braid, blue for
  quilt edge   5¼ yards
Edging, 3½"-wide,
  white eyelet   5¼ yards
Embroidery floss: blue
                     light green
                     white
Fabric glue stick
Quilting thread   blue
⅜"-wide blue satin
  ribbon   3¾ yards
⅜"-wide white satin
  ribbon   3¾ yards
Ribbon rosettes   4 white
Seed pearls

Number to Cut
Template A   3 light blue
Template A rev.   2 light blue
Template B   1 light blue
Template B rev.   1 light blue
Template C   1 light blue
Template D   1 light blue

Quilt Top Assembly
1. Cut a 38½" x 53½" rectangle from white. Finger-crease rectangle in half twice to find center. Lightly mark the **Bouquet Design** in center of rectangle with pencil. (See quilt photograph.) Mark single flower design in each of the lower

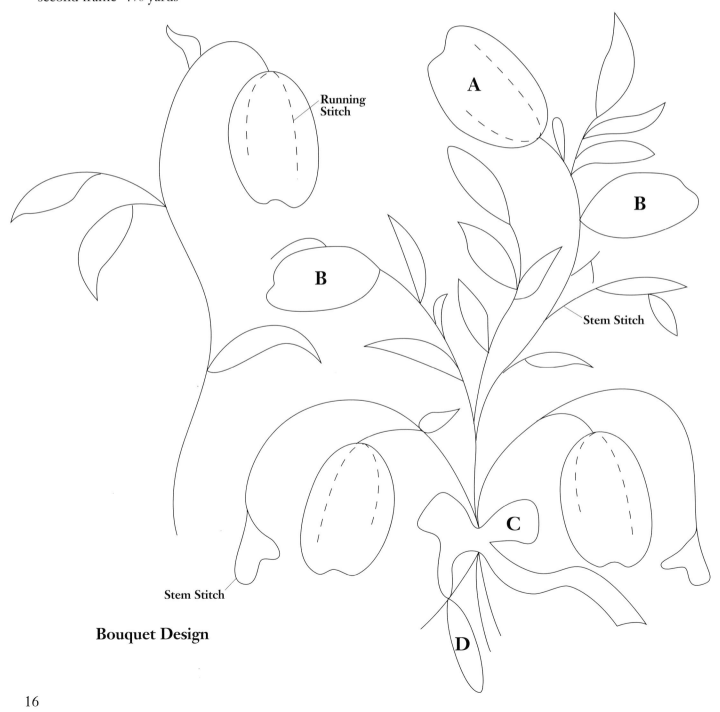

Running
Stitch

Stem Stitch

Stem Stitch

Bouquet Design

corners, as shown in quilt photograph. Mark oval, framing areas, all feather plumes, and ribbon cable quilting patterns, as shown in **Setting** and **Quilting Diagrams**.

2. Position flower and ribbon pieces on rectangle and anchor them, using glue stick. Cut a 38½" x 53½" rectangle from voile and carefully place it over the rectangle and pieces. Smooth voile repeatedly in every direction and baste in place. Since voile will stretch and give easily, it is important to baste it heavily in place.

3. Using 1 strand of blue embroidery floss, outline-stitch *inside* the edge of center bouquet pieces through voile and white fabric. Referring to **Bouquet Design**, embellish flowers with running stitches. Using 3 strands of light green embroidery floss, stemstitch stems and leaves.

Quilting

1. Because of the unstable nature of voile, prepare the quilt for quilting (see **Layering and Basting**, page 10) immediately after completing the center bouquet. Begin quilting from the bouquet outward, stopping several inches from the corner bouquets.

Using white quilting thread, background-quilt oval in a ¼" diagonal cross-hatching pattern. Begin echo-quilting at oval's outside edge, and quilt 9 lines, ¼" apart, as shown in **Quilting Diagram** and quilt photograph. Quilt feather plumes. Echo-quilt from inside first frame with lines of quilting, ¼" apart. Quilt remainder of area inside first frame in diagonal parallel lines, ½" apart.

2. Quilt area between first frame and second frame in a ½" diagonal cross-hatching pattern, remembering to stop quilting several inches from corner bouquets.

Shadow-appliqué corner bouquets by carefully placing stitches so that the floss passes through the voile, pattern piece, and white fabric *only*. Embellish pieces, as shown in **Bouquet Design**. Complete quilting of second frame.

3. Using 3 strands of white embroidery floss, work a running stitch inside marked lines of ribbon cable quilting pattern *through voile and white fabric only*. Quilt the ribbon cable using blue quilting thread.

4. Using white quilting thread, outline-quilt outside edges of all flowers and ribbon.

5. When stitching is complete, soak shadow-appliquéd areas for a few minutes in water to remove glue.

Finished Edges

With right sides facing and raw edges aligned, stitch eyelet edging to quilt top only and miter corners. (See quilt photograph.) Turn under raw edges of top and backing to meet. Trim batting, if necessary.

Blindstitch folded edges together. Referring to photograph, hand-stitch blue braid to edges of *quilt top only*; attach a ribbon rosette to each corner.

Braid and Ribbon Attachment

Carefully hand-stitch braid with flower design to *quilt top only* along lines of oval. (See quilt photograph.) Hand-stitch seed pearls in the center of each flower of the braid. Hand-stitch white braid to quilt top for first frame, as shown in **Setting Diagram** and quilt photograph. Hand-stitch white braid to quilt top for second frame, as shown in **Setting Diagram,** and quilt photograph.

Make a bow using white and blue ribbons, leaving long streamers. (Do not cut ribbon yardage until placement is final.) Pin bow to right upper corner, as shown in quilt photograph. Take left-hand streamers and drape them across quilt, as shown. Carefully twist and turn streamers as you go, in a loose and flowing manner, and pin in place. Make bow for left upper corner. Arrange streamers down the sides of quilt, twisting and turning ribbons as before, until a pleasing arrangement is reached. Tack ribbon with seed pearls, being careful not to stitch through to the backing.

Setting Diagram

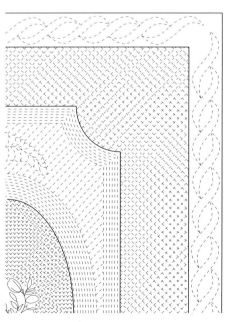

Quilting Diagram

Quilt by Susan Jung
Manhattan Beach, California

Country Garden

Combine flowered chintz with the speed of rotary cutting, and you have a quick-and-easy quilt that's sweet enough to wrap a precious cherub.

Finished Quilt Size
44" x 54"

Number of Blocks and Finished Size
12 blocks   10" square

Fabric Requirements
Light floral chintz   ¾ yard
Dark floral chintz   ¾ yard
Light chintz for borders   1¼ yards
Dark chintz for borders   1⅜ yards
Backing   1⅝ yards

Other Materials
3½ yards (⅜"-wide) satin ribbon in
     assorted colors
Yarn needle

Number to Cut*
Template A   48 light floral chintz
                  48 dark floral chintz

*See alternate rotary cutting method.

Quilt Top Assembly

1. To cut pieces using rotary cutter, cut ¾ yard lengths of light and dark chintz into 5½"-wide strips. Cut each color of strips into 24 (5½") squares. Cut squares in half diagonally. You should have a total of 48 light triangles and 48 dark triangles. Referring to **Block Assembly Diagram**, join 1 light and 1 dark triangle along bias edge to form a square. Join 4 pieced squares to form 1 block. Repeat to make 12 blocks.

2. Follow **Quilt Top Assembly Diagram** to join blocks in 4 horizontal rows of 3 blocks each. Join rows.

3. Cut 4 (1½"-wide) border strips from dark chintz and join to quilt as shown in **Quilt Top Assembly Diagram**. Cut 4 (3½"-wide) border strips from light chintz and join to quilt. Cut 4 (3½"-wide) border strips from dark chintz and join to quilt.

4. Layer batting; top, right side up; and backing, right side down. With batting against feed dogs, join layers along sides and bottom. Turn through opening, with batting on inside. Slipstitch opening closed.

5. Cut ribbon into 20 (6") pieces. Beginning at center of quilt, tie bows at all block corners as follows: Thread yarn needle with 1 (6") length of ribbon. Sew ribbon through all thicknesses and tie on top. (See photograph.) Machine-quilt in-the-ditch between borders.

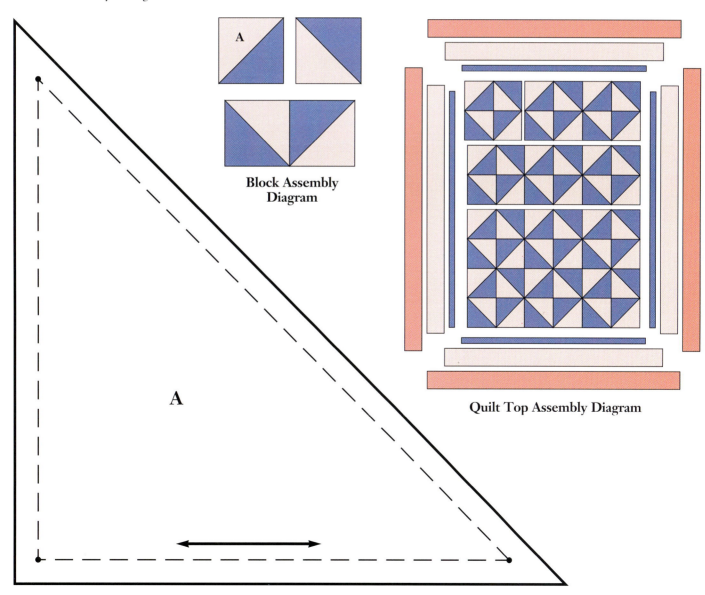

Block Assembly Diagram

Quilt Top Assembly Diagram

Quilt by Katy J. Widger
Los Lunas, New Mexico

Child's Play

Is there a budding young artist in your life whose drawings are too special to throw away? Ask the child to draw pictures using heat transfer crayons. Through a simple process, described here, you can transfer the drawings to fabric and incorporate into a quilt. Fabrics with heat-transfer crayon imprints can be washed in warm water and a mild detergent on gentle cycle. Do not use bleach or place the quilt in the dryer.

Finished Quilt Size

53½" x 53½"

Number of Blocks and Finished Size

9 blocks   16" x 16"

Fabric Requirements

White*	1½ yards
Border print**	2½ yards
Pink	1½ yards
8 prints†	¼ yard each
8 solids†	¼ yard each
Backing	3¼ yards

*Select a cotton/polyester blend and wash fabric before transferring drawings. See step 2.

**Select a bright-colored print to match crayon colors. Yardage for bias binding is included.

†Prints and solids are used for framing strips. Select colors to match crayon colors.

Other Materials

Heat transfer crayons
Newspapers
Machine embroidery threads, variegated and to match backing for machine quilting
White butcher paper

Number to Cut

13" square	9 butcher paper
	9 white
2¼" x 22½" strip	36 prints
	36 solids
5" x 14" rectangle	24 border print
	24 pink

Quilt Top Assembly

1. Center and draw a 12½" square on each butcher paper square. (The drawn square serves as a boundary for the drawings.)

Have the child draw pictures using heat transfer crayons. The child should press very firmly with the crayons and cover the entire 12½" square.

2. Place a stack of newspapers on ironing board and top stack with a clean sheet of butcher paper. Lay white square on top of paper stack.

Brush excess crayon specks from each drawing. Lay 1 drawing face down on top of white square, matching edges. Place another clean sheet of butcher paper on top of drawing.

Using a dry iron set on "cotton," apply steady pressure over entire drawing until drawing becomes slightly visible through back of papers. Lift iron from place to place, because sliding it across surface may blur image.

Carefully separate drawing from white square. (Drawing can be reused if more crayon is applied.) Repeat for each drawing. Trim each white square to 12½".

3. Using Log Cabin piecing technique, join 1 round of framing strips to each square, as shown in **Skewed Log Cabin Frame Diagram, Figure 1**. Begin with a solid strip joined to top of square and alternate joining solids and print strips in a clockwise direction, as shown. (See quilt photograph.)

Stop after fourth strip is joined.

Measure and mark 1¾" from square seam line across framing strip 1 at left and 1¼" at right, as shown in **Skewed Log Cabin Frame Diagram, Figure 2**. Connect marks, drawing a line over framing strips at an angle. Trim along line. Join a print framing strip to new edge.

Repeat for remaining sides, as shown in **Skewed Log Cabin Frame, Figure 3**.

When round 2 strips have been joined, trim framing strips to make a 16½" block. (See **Skewed Log Cabin Frame, Figure 4**.)

Repeat for each square.

4. Arrange blocks in 3 rows of 3 blocks each. Join blocks at sides to form rows and join rows.

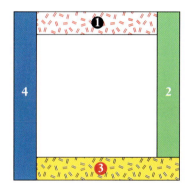

Figure 1

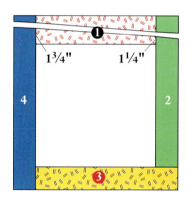

Figure 2

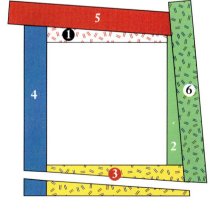

Figure 3

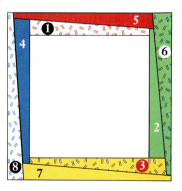

Figure 4

Skewed Log Cabin Frame Diagram

5. Group 5" x 14" rectangles in sets of 4: 2 border print and 2 pink. With raw edges aligned, stack rectangle sets and cut across them at random angles to form wedges. Wedges should be cut wide enough to include seam allowances so that finished pieces do not come to a point. (See pieces after joining in **Border Piecing Diagram, Figure 1.**)

Alternate 2 border print wedges with 2 pink pieces from 1 stack, as shown in **Border Piecing Diagram, Figure 1,** and join to form units. (When joining wedges from the same stack, they will fit together and form rectangles. Therefore, little fabric is wasted.) Cut across units to make 4 segments, as shown in **Border Piecing Diagram, Figure 2.** (Again, cut segments wide enough to include seam allowances so that finished pieces do not come to a point.) Repeat until all wedges have been joined and segments cut.

Alternate segments in random manner and join to make 4 long strips for borders. Trim long edges even so that each strip is 3¼" wide. (See **Border Piecing Diagram, Figure 3.**) Join borders to opposite sides of quilt.

Join remaining borders to top and bottom of quilt.

Quilting

Using variegated thread in top spool and a thread color to match backing in bobbin, machine-quilt selected areas of each drawing.

Use a ⅛"-wide and 12-stitch-length zigzag stitch to quilt over seams of block framing strips.

Finished Edges

Bind with border print.

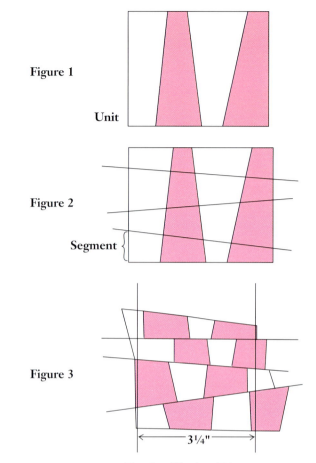

Figure 1

Unit

Figure 2

Segment

Figure 3

3¼"

Border Piecing Diagram

Quilt by Kim A. Christensen-Kent
Racine, Wisconsin

Amish Homage

The soft flannel backing and the bright, crisp colors of this quilt make it irresistible to any infant. *Amish Homage* is a contemporary version of the traditional Amish Shadows or Roman Stripe pattern.

Finished Quilt Size

37" x 37"

Number of Blocks and Finished Size

16 blocks   9" x 9"

Fabric Requirements

Green	¾ yard
White	¾ yard
Orange	¾ yard
Pink	¾ yard
Red	¾ yard
Yellow	¾ yard
Blue	¾ yard
Lavender	¾ yard
White flannel for backing	1¼ yards

Number to Cut

Template A	2 green
	1 white
	4 orange
	2 pink
	3 red
	3 yellow
	1 blue
Template B	1 green
	2 white
	3 orange
	3 pink
	4 red
	2 yellow
	1 lavender
Template C	3 white
	2 orange
	4 pink
	3 red
	1 yellow
	1 blue
	2 lavender
Template D	1 green
	4 white
	1 orange
	3 pink
	2 red
	2 blue
	3 lavender
Template E	2 green
	3 white
	2 pink
	1 red
	1 yellow
	3 blue
	4 lavender
Template F	3 green
	2 white
	1 orange
	1 pink
	2 yellow
	4 blue
	3 lavender
Template G	4 green
	1 white
	2 orange
	1 red
	3 yellow
	3 blue
	2 lavender
Right triangle (9" on sides, finished size)	3 green
	3 orange
	1 pink
	2 red
	4 yellow
	2 blue
	1 lavender

Quilt Top Assembly

1. Join Templates (A–F) lengthwise and Template G, alternating colors as shown in quilt photograph to form a pieced triangle. Repeat to make 16.

2. Join solid triangles to pieced triangles along bias edge to form squares. Make 16 squares.

3. Join 4 squares at sides to form a row, as shown in quilt photograph. Make 4 rows and join rows.

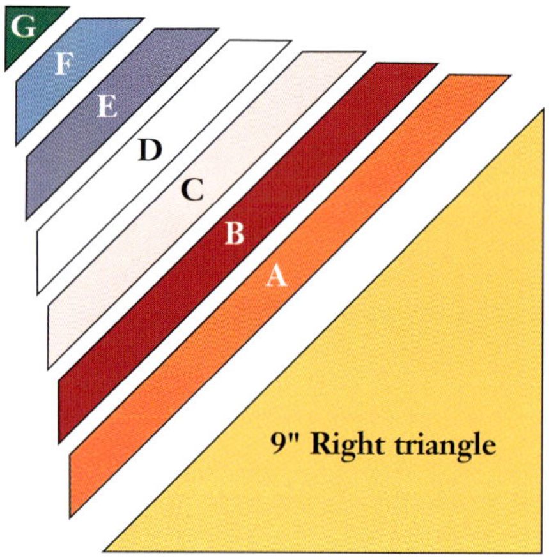

Block Assembly Diagram

Quilting

Quilt diagonal lines the length of quilt, 1¼" apart, in the direction opposite to the lengthwise seams of pieced triangles.

Finished Edges

Turn 1" of flannel backing to front and miter corners. Turn raw edge under ¼" and blindstitch to quilt.

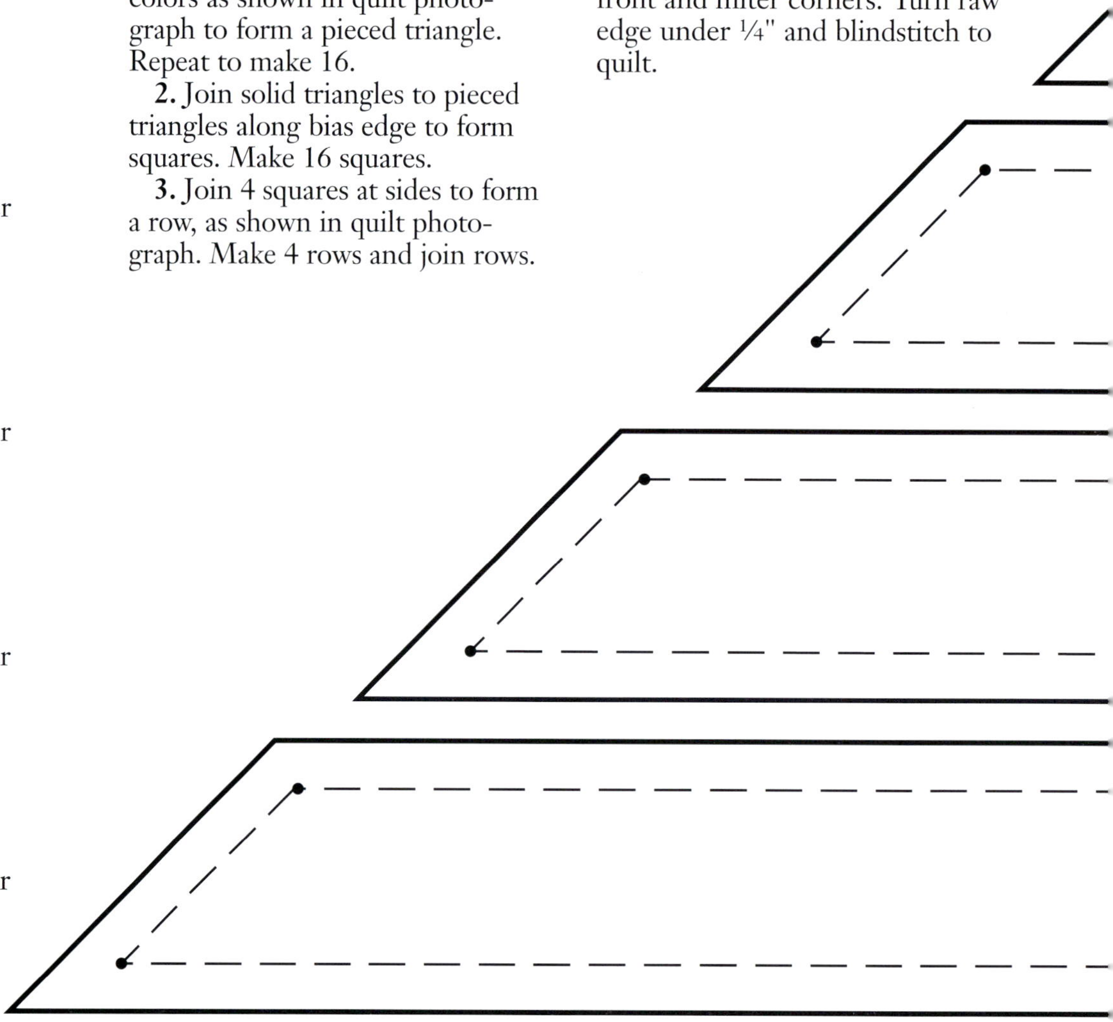

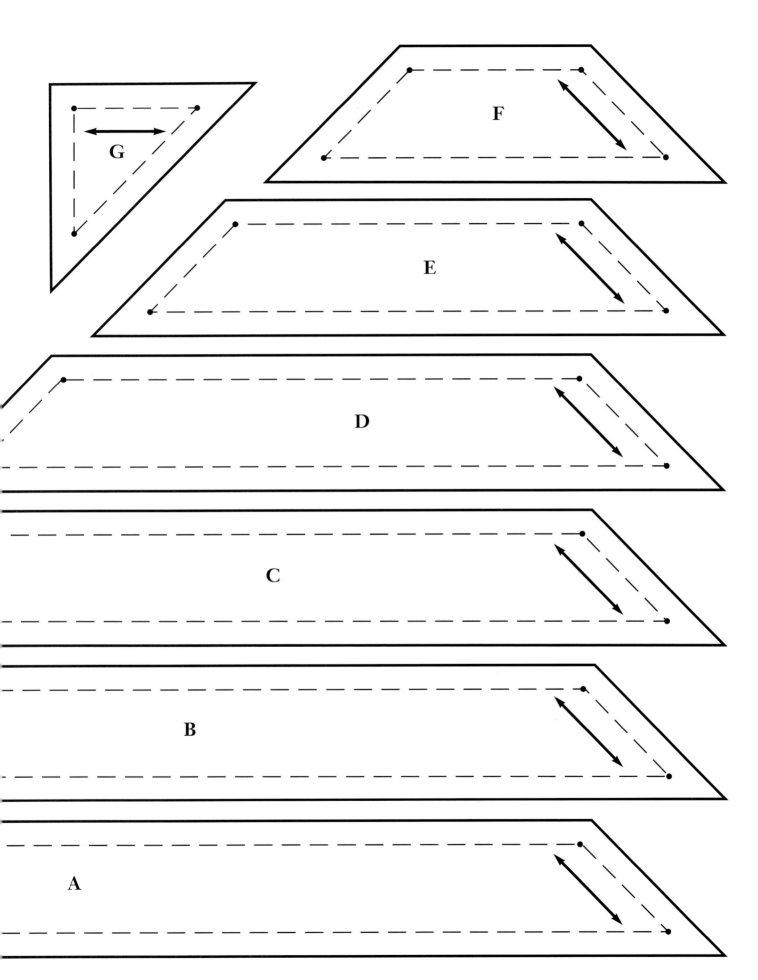

Quilt by Dorothy R. Winkeljohn
Fairborn, Ohio

Calico Strings

The pieced print panels that highlight this nursery quilt are made using string piecing and the quilt-as-you-piece method. Choose prints from your scrap bag, or purchase coordinating fabrics in the color scheme of your choice to make this sturdy quick quilt that's designed to last for generations.

Finished Quilt Size
36" x 44½"

Fabric Requirements
Blue print* 3⅛ yards
Assorted prints 1¼ yards

*Includes sashing, borders, backing, and
 binding.

Number to Cut
6½" x 39" panel 4 blue print
       4 batting
2½" x 39" strip 6 blue print
       3 batting
3½" x 39" strip 8 blue print
       4 batting

Quilt Top Assembly
1. Cut assorted prints into cross-wise strings of varying widths, ranging from 1¾" to 2¾".

2. Baste 1 (6½" x 39") batting panel to wrong side of 1 (6½" x 39") blue print backing panel. Following **String-Pieced Panels Diagram**, lay 1 print string, right side up, diagonally across top right corner of batting. Trim and add excess to remaining strings. With right sides facing and raw edges aligned, lay second string on top of first. Trim and reserve excess as before. Join through all layers as shown in **Figure 1**. Flip String 2 over and finger-press as shown in **Figure 2**. Lay a third string on top of String 2 and join as before. Repeat until entire panel is covered. Trim strings even with backing panel. Repeat to make 1 more string-pieced panel.

Repeat Step 2 to make 2 more panels, this time beginning string piecing in top left corner, for a total of 4 panels.

3. Refer to **Quilt-As-You-Piece Diagram** to attach 1 (2½" x 39") blue print sashing strip to 1 string-pieced panel as follows: With raw edges aligned, layer back sashing strip, wrong side down; strip-pieced panel, backing side down; front sashing strip, right side down; and 1 (2½" x 39") piece of batting. Baste all layers together. With batting against feed dogs, stitch along seam line as indicated. Trim batting from seam allowance.

Quilt Assembly Diagram

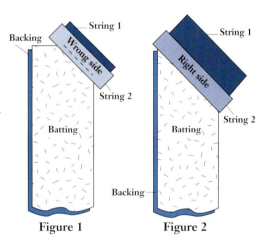

Figure 1   Figure 2

String-Pieced Panels Diagram

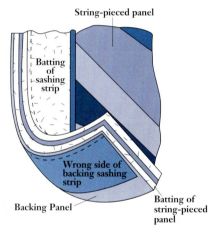

Quilt-As-You-Piece Diagram

Fold sashing strips and batting outward. Topstitch ¼" from seam line on top sashing strip. (See **Quilt Assembly Diagram**.)

Place right side of second string-pieced panel facing right side of the top sashing strip that you just joined to the first string-pieced panel. Join second string-pieced panel to top sashing strip and batting, stitching ¼" from edge. Trim excess batting from seam. Press seam toward sashing strip. Turn under ¼" on bottom sashing strip and whipstitch in place. Topstitch ¼" from seam line on top sashing strip.

Repeat Step 3 to join remaining string-pieced panels and sashing strips.

4. Trim 4 of the 3½" x 39" blue print border strips and 2 of the 3½" x 39" batting strips to match sides of quilt and join to sides of quilt using quilt-as-you-piece method. Trim remaining border and batting strips and join to top and bottom of quilt using quilt-as-you-piece method. Topstitch ¼" from edge of strip-pieced panels on border all around quilt. (See **Quilt Assembly Diagram**.)

5. Round off corners of quilt, using small plate or French curve.

Finished Edges
Bind with bias binding made from remaining blue print.

Quilt by Sylvia Whitesides
Lafayette, Indiana

Ryan's Quilt

Cross-stitched lambs, ducks, and hearts add more
cheer to this special quilt. It serves well as crib quilt
or wall hanging.

Finished Quilt Size
40" x 40"

Number of Blocks and Finished Size
61 nine-patch
  blocks   3" x 3"

Fabric Requirements
Light blue (LB)   ½ yard
Medium blue print (MBP) ½ yard
Medium blue (MB)   ½ yard
Rose print (R)   ½ yard
Dark blue print (DB)   1½ yards
Dark blue print for
  bias binding   1 yard
Backing   1½ yards

Other Materials
14-count Aida   ½ yard
DMC embroidery floss:
  #931 antique blue-medium
  #316 antique mauve-medium
  #930 antique blue-dark
  #902 garnet-very dark
  #613 drab brown-light

Number to Cut
Template A   140 light blue
             133 rose print
             140 medium blue
                print
             176 dark blue print
Template B   32 light blue
Template C   24 dark blue print
Template D   4 dark blue print

Quilt Top Assembly
  1. Refer to **Cross-stitching Charts** and make number indicated.
  2. Using As, Bs, and cross-stitched squares, make the appropriate number of units, as shown in **Color Code Charts for Units**. Note placement of cross-stitched squares.

Cross-stitching Charts

Cross-stitch (2 strands).
  ⊠ 931 antique blue-medium
  ⊡ 316 antique mauve-medium
  ⊞ 902 garnet-very dark
  ⊟ 930 antique blue-dark
  ⊡ 613 drab brown-light

Backstitch (1 strand)
  ⊘ 931 antique blue-medium

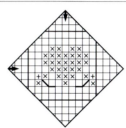

Heart
Make 20 (total) for Units 3, 4, 5, and 6.
Cross-stitch on a 1½" diamond.

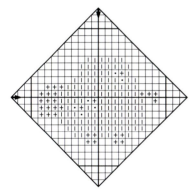

Sheep
Make 8 for Unit 10.
Cross-stitch on a 2½" diamond.

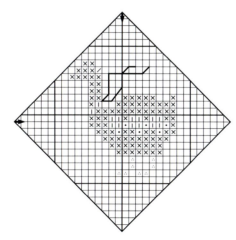

Duck
Make 8 for Unit 9.
Cross-stitch on a 2½" diamond.

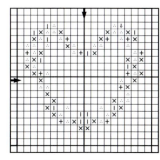

Corner Heart
Make 4.
Cross-stitch on a 2½" square.

Heart
Make 4 for Unit 8.
Cross-stitch on a 1½" square.

Color Code Charts for Units

  LB — Light blue
MBP — Medium
        blue print
  DB — Dark blue
        print
  R — Rose print

Unit 1:
Make 16.

Unit 2:
Make 9.

Unit 3:
Make 6.

Unit 4:
Make 6.

Unit 5:
Make 2.

Unit 6:
Make 2.

Unit 7:
Make 20.

Unit 8:
Make 4.

Unit 9:
Make 8.

Unit 10:
Make 8.

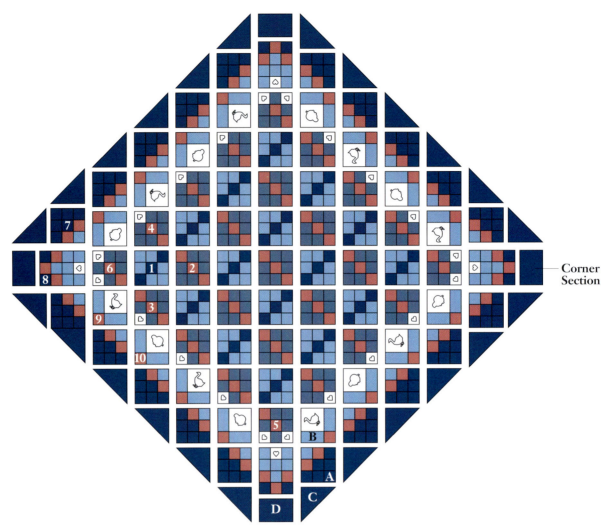

Setting Diagram

3. Referring to **Setting Diagram**, arrange units as shown. Join units at sides to form rows, adding Cs at each end. Join Ds to end of unit 8s, Cs to unit 7s as shown, and join to form corner sections. Join rows to complete medallion. Trim outside edges to ¼" seam allowance.

4. Set medallion on point and cut right triangles from dark blue print for medallion sides. Join bias edges of triangles to sides of medallion.

5. Cut 2 rose print strips, 2 dark blue print strips, and 8 medium blue strips, 1½" wide, across fabric. Make combination strips of 3 strips each, by joining strips lengthwise as follows: medium blue, rose print, and medium blue; medium blue, dark blue print, and medium blue.

Cut strips, 1½" wide, across seam lines of joined strips. Join strips, alternating rose print and dark blue print strips, as shown in **Border Piecing Diagram**. Make 4 border strips.

Border Piecing Diagram

Referring to **Corner Piecing Diagram**, join 1 medium blue square to each end of all 4 strips as shown. In preparation for corner piece, join this square by stitching from outside edge to center seam line and backstitching 1 or 2 stitches. Trim edges of squares to ¼"

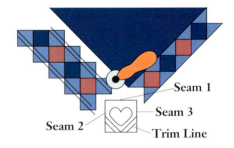

Corner Piecing Diagram

seam allowance on top and bottom, as shown in **Border Piecing** and **Corner Piecing Diagrams**. Join strips to quilt.

Set cross-stitched heart in each corner. (See **Corner Piecing Diagram**.) Stitch seam 1, beginning and ending at the seam line and backstitching 1 or 2 stitches at beginning and end. Remove fabric from the machine. Align the raw

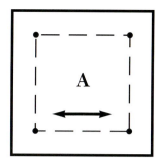

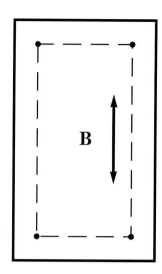

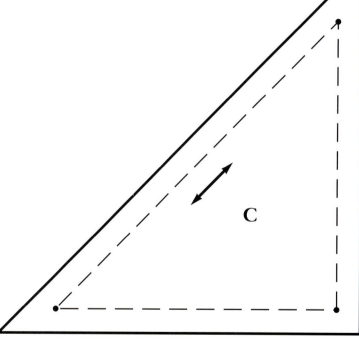

edges of seam 2 and stitch from the center to the outside edge, back-stitching 1 or 2 stitches at the start. Repeat for seam 3. Trim corner edges even with border strips.

Quilting

Quilt in-the-ditch around rose and dark blue print medallion squares. Quilt a feathered heart in each corner. The remainder of the corner area is quilted in a 1" cross-hatching pattern to blend with the medallion quilting. Quilt in-the-ditch of border squares.

Finished Edges

Bind with a continuous bias strip of dark blue print.

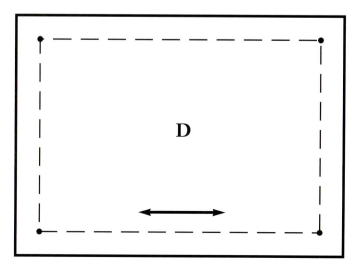

Quilt by Carol Logan Newbill
Birmingham, Alabama
Quilt owned by Melinda Ponder Goode

Welcome, Sunshine

Combine appliqué with traditional pieced blocks to
make this happy baby quilt. It's a charming way to greet
a much-loved bundle of sunshine.

Finished Quilt Size
48" x 48"

Number of Blocks and Finished Size
36 blocks   6" x 6"

Fabric Requirements*

Gold	1½ yards
Pink	1 yard
Blue	1 yard
Backing	3¼ yards
Gold for bias binding	¾ yard

*See Step 1 to cut borders and corner squares before cutting other pieces.

Other Materials
1 skein brown embroidery floss

Number to Cut

Template A	20 pink
	12 blue
Template B	4 gold
	8 pink
	20 blue
Template C	4 gold
Template D	4 gold
Template E	8 gold

Quilt Top Assembly

1. From gold, cut 4 (6½" x 48½") strips for borders. From blue, cut 4 (6½") corner squares. Set borders and squares aside.

2. Set 4 blue As aside for center. Referring to **Quilt Top Assembly Diagram**, Step 1, for color placement, join remaining pink and blue As and Bs to make 28 blocks. Join blocks, corner squares, and 4 blue center As as shown, leaving a hole for sunshine at center.

3. Referring to **Quilt Top Assembly Diagram**, Step 2, appliqué Cs, Ds, and Es around center hole as shown, aligning raw edges.

4. Join 4 gold Bs along straight edges to form circle. Transfer face markings to circle. Using 3 strands of brown floss, embroider face as indicated. Appliqué circle over center hole to complete sunshine, as shown in **Quilt Top Assembly Diagram**, Step 3.

5. Join border strips to edges of quilt, mitering corners, using Template B to round corners as shown in **Border Diagram**.

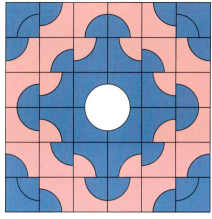

Step 1

Step 2

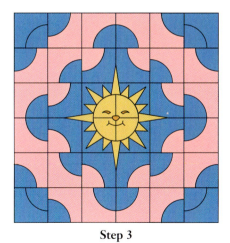

Step 3

Quilt Top Assembly Diagram

Quilting
Quilt as desired.

Finished Edges
Bind with bias binding made from gold.

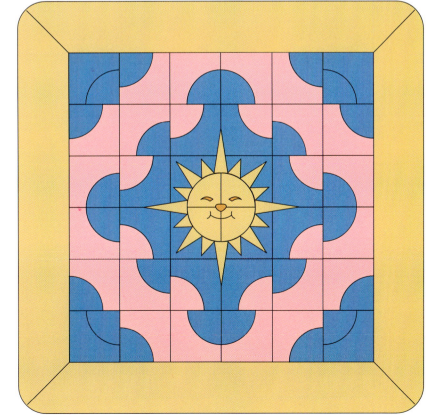

Border Diagram

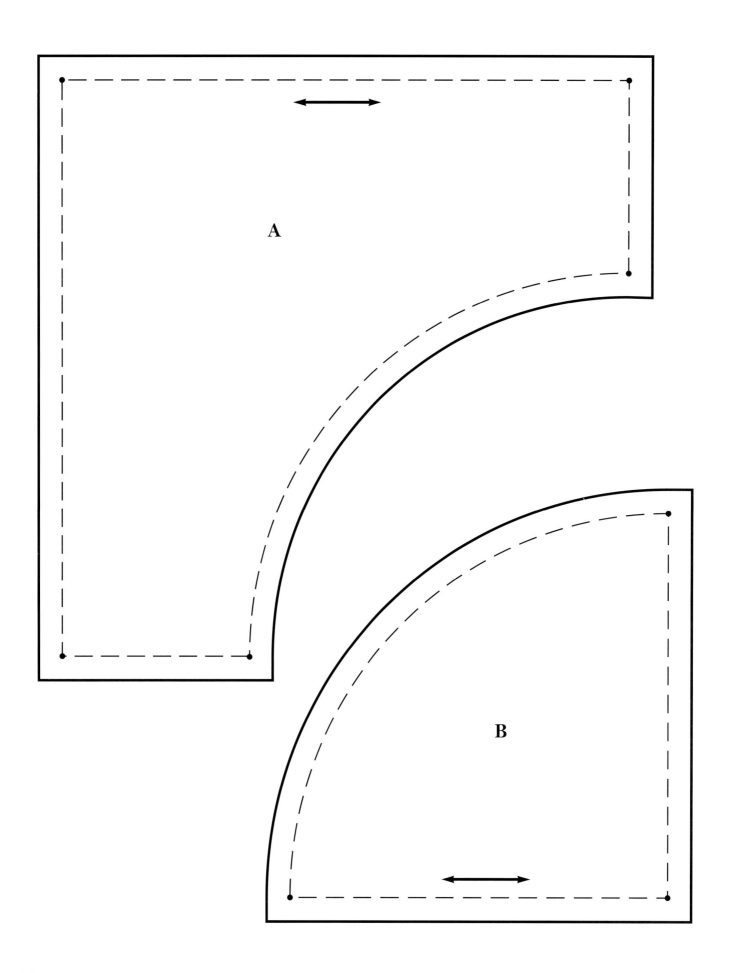

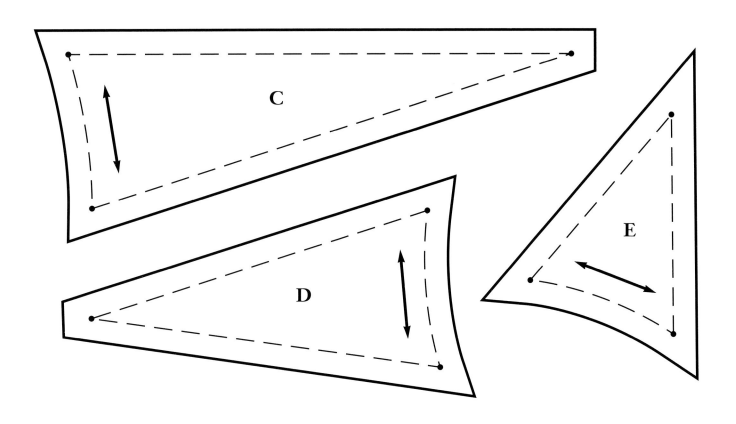

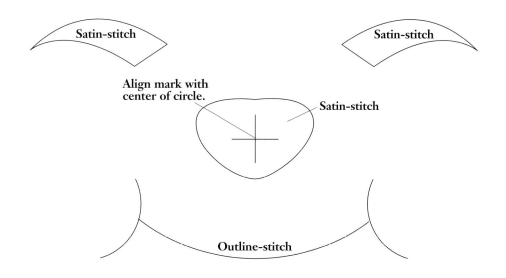

Satin-stitch

Satin-stitch

Align mark with
center of circle.

Satin-stitch

Outline-stitch

Face Markings

Quilt by Kimberly McKeough
Fredericksburg, Virginia

Arizona Spring

Need a quick baby shower gift? This quilt stitches up in no time because of the fast machine-piecing method used to make it.

Finished Quilt Size

37" x 56¼"

Fabric Requirements

Pink solid	1½ yards
Dark paisley print	1¾ yards
Assorted dark prints	¾ yard
Assorted light prints	¾ yard
Blue print	⅜ yard
Backing	1⅞ yards
Burgundy print for binding	¾ yard

Quilt Top Assembly

1. Cut 4 (1½"-wide) lengthwise strips from pink solid and 4 (3½"-wide) lengthwise strips from paisley. Set aside for borders. Cut a 22" square from paisley and set aside to make bias binding. Add remaining paisley to assorted dark prints.

2. Cut light and dark prints into 2"-wide crosswise strips. Cut strips into 84 (2" x 6") dark rectangles and 84 (2" x 6") light rectangles.

From blue print, cut 2 (8½") squares. Cut these squares into quarters diagonally to make 8 quarter-square triangles. Set aside 7 of the triangles for use as large triangles. (See **Quilt Top Assembly Diagram.**) Cut remaining quarter-square triangle in half to make 2 triangles with 6" bases. Set these aside for use as small triangles. (See **Quilt Top Assembly Diagram.**)

From remaining blue print, cut 44 (2") squares. From remaining pink solid, cut 40 (2") squares.

Quilt Top Assembly Diagram

3. Referring to photograph for color placement, follow **Diagram 1** to join 1 (2") square to 1 (2" x 6") rectangle. (*Note*: Square/rectangle strip is on left side of row.) Repeat for a total of 84 square/rectangle strips.

4. Referring to photograph for color placement, follow **Diagram 2** to join 1 rectangle to right side of 1 large triangle (unit 1 in Diagram). Join 1 square/rectangle strip (unit 2 in Diagram) to left side of unit 1. Join 1 rectangle (unit 3) to right side of row. Continue, joining square/rectangle strips to left side and rectangles to right side as shown in **Diagram 2** until you have built a row of 21 chevrons. Repeat to make a total of 4 rows.

5. Join rows as shown in **Diagram 3** and **Quilt Top Assembly Diagram**. (*Note:* Because rows are all bias-cut and bias edges stretch easily, be very careful and pin frequently when joining sides of rows.) Trim edges of rows as indicated in **Diagram 3**.

6. Refer to **Quilt Top Assembly Diagram** to join 3 large triangles and 2 small triangles to top of quilt.

7. Join pink inner borders to quilt, mitering corners. Join the paisley outer borders to quilt, mitering corners.

Quilting

Refer to photograph for suggested quilting.

Finished Edges

Bind with a continuous strip of bias binding made from 22" paisley square.

Diagram 1

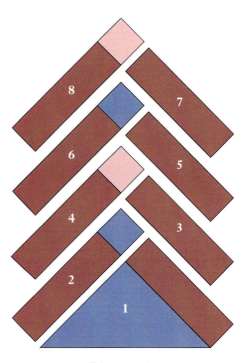

Diagram 2

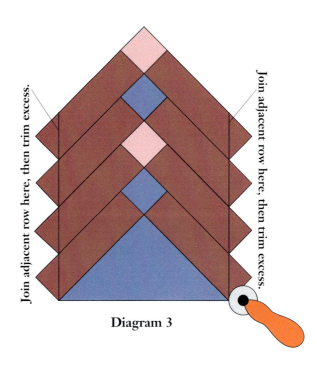

Join adjacent row here, then trim excess.

Join adjacent row here, then trim excess.

Diagram 3

Quilt by Carol M. Tipton
Calera, Alabama

Noah's Star

Celebrate the promise of hope with this Bible story quilt framed in rainbow prairie points. Use simple outline stitch to embroider Noah and his friends into the star blocks.

Finished Quilt Size
58" x 58"

Number of Blocks and Finished Size
4 blocks   18" square

Fabric Requirements
Blue   2 yards
Rainbow stripe   1¾ yards
White   1¾ yards
Backing   3¼ yards

Other Materials
4 skeins blue embroidery floss
Tracing paper (optional)

Number to Cut
6½" x 19" strip	2 blue
6½" x 43" strip	1 blue
6¾" x 43" strip	2 blue
6¾" x 55" strip	2 blue
Template B	32 blue
	16 rainbow stripe
	16 white
10" square	20 white
5" square	80 stripe

Quilt Top Assembly

1. Trace 1 embroidery pattern onto each white square, centering design on square. Trace 1 each of Noah, ark, sun, and dove designs. Trace 1 of each animal with pattern face up and 1 of each animal with pattern face down to make mirror-image units.

2. Using 3 strands of embroidery floss, embroider all traced lines in outline stitch. Make eyes and other details with satin stitch or French knots, if desired. Remove any visible markings. Lightly press blocks.

3. Center Template A on each embroidered block; trim excess fabric. If you prefer, use an acrylic ruler with a rotary cutter instead of the template to trim blocks.

4. Join white Bs to blue Bs, matching short sides as shown in **Diagram 1**. Repeat to join striped Bs and remaining blue Bs. Press all seam allowances toward blue.

5. Referring to **Diagram 1,** join 2 triangle units to make a pieced square. Repeat to make 16 squares.

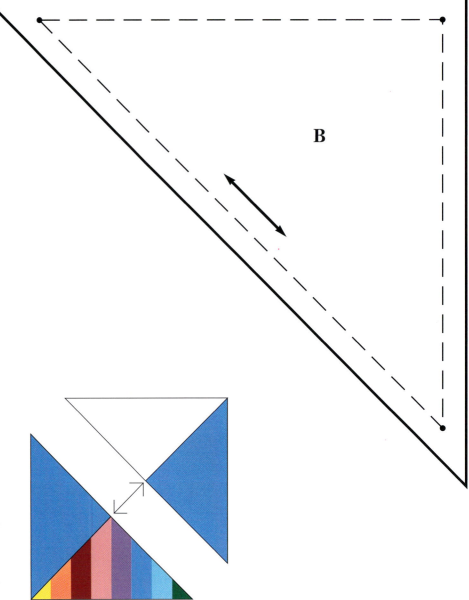

Diagram 1

6. Arrange 4 pieced squares with 5 embroidered squares, referring to photograph for placement. Note that each block has the same animal in opposite corners. Join squares to complete each block.

7. Join 2 blocks with 1 (6½" x 19") blue sashing strip between them. Repeat for remaining 2 blocks. Press seam allowances toward sashing. Trim sashing even with blocks.

8. Stitch the 2 sections together with 6½" x 43" blue sashing strip between them.

9. Stitch 1 (6¾" x 43") blue border strip each to top and bottom edges; then stitch 1 (6¾" x 55") blue border strip each to side edges.

Quilting

Referring to photograph, transfer **Wave Quilting Pattern** to outer borders, adjusting at corners as necessary. Transfer **Rainbow Quilting Pattern** to center sashing, adjusting as necessary to connect rainbow lines at intersection of sashing strips.

Quilt on all marked lines. In blocks, outline quilt ¼" from each seam line.

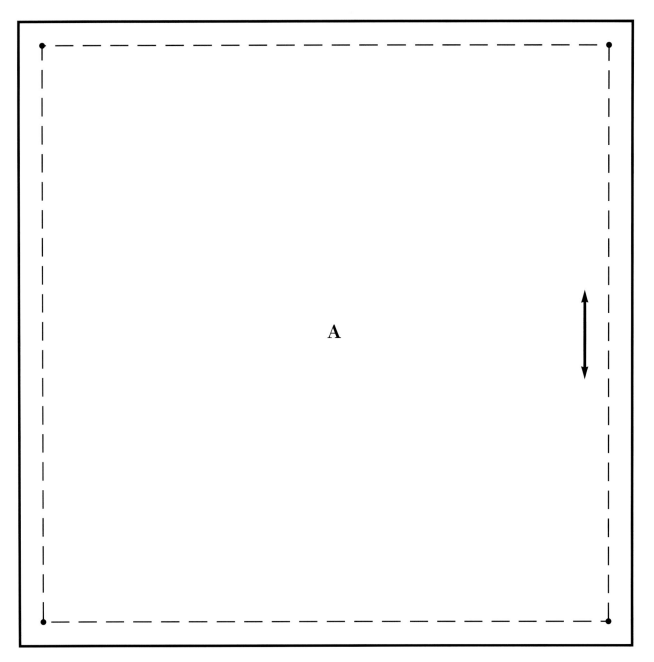

A

Finished Edges

Referring to **Diagram 2**, fold each stripe square in half twice to make a small triangle. Press.

With right sides facing and raw edges aligned, pin 16 to 18 triangles to each quilt top edge. Space triangles evenly, starting at a corner and overlapping adjacent points as shown in **Diagram 3**.

When satisfied with spacing, stitch triangles in place with a ½" seam **(Diagram 4)**.

Press triangles to right side. Trim batting if necessary. Fold under a ½" hem on backing to cover raw edges of triangles. Blindstitch in place **(Diagram 5)**.

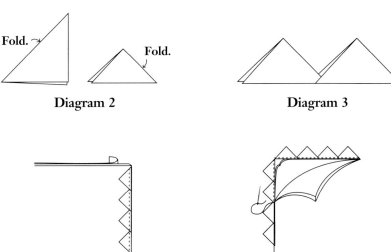

Fold. →

Fold.

Diagram 2

Diagram 3

Diagram 4

Diagram 5

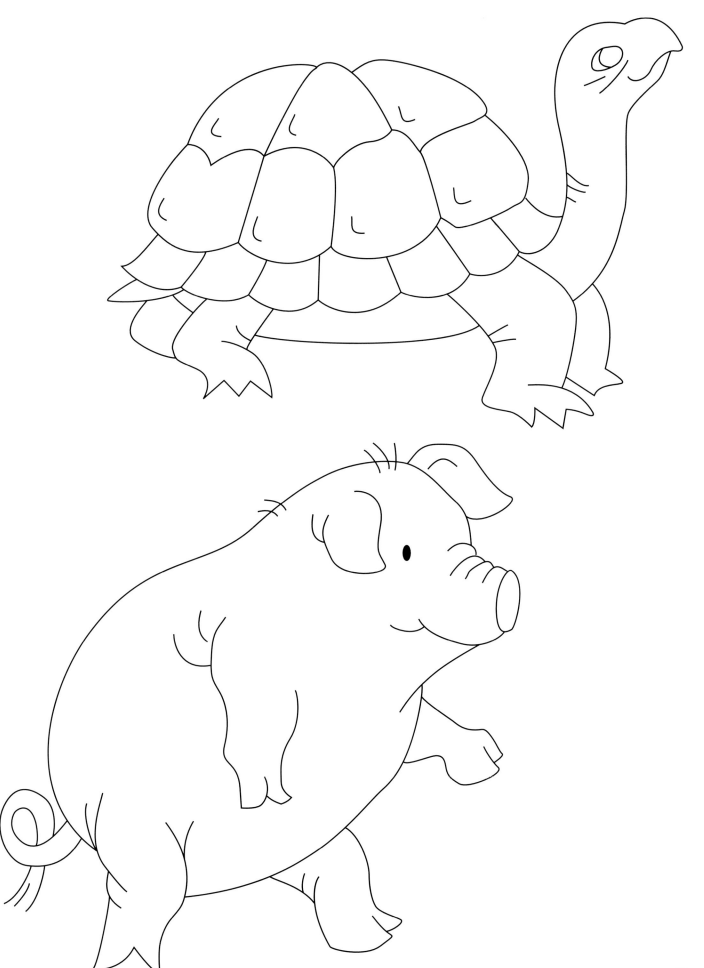

Rainbow Quilting Pattern

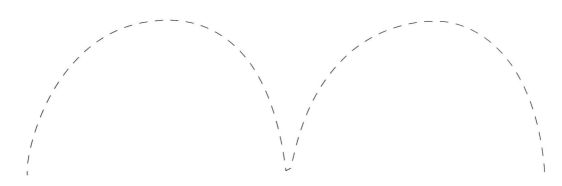

Wave Quilting Pattern